# MAKING FLOWERS *from* WOOL

**NAN LONCHARICH**

*Illustrations by Kim Kiser*
*Photographs by Alan Wycheck*

**STACKPOLE BOOKS**

Copyright © 2011 by Stackpole Books

Published by
STACKPOLE BOOKS
5067 Ritter Road
Mechanicsburg, PA 17055
www.stackpolebooks.com

Printed in the United States of America

10  9  8  7  6  5  4  3  2  1

First edition

Cover design by Tessa J. Sweigert

**Library of Congress Cataloging-in-Publication Data**

Loncharich, Nan.
 Making flowers from wool / Nan Loncharich ; illustrations
by Kim Kiser ; photographs by Alan Wycheck. — 1st ed.
  p. cm.
 ISBN 978-0-8117-0758-9
 1. Fabric flowers. 2. Felt work. 3. Wool fabrics. I. Title.
 TT890.5.L66 2011
 746'.0463—dc22

                    2010053885

# Contents

# Introduction

**W**elcome.

If you're like me, you have old wool clothing packed away in storage, as well as wool fabric scraps left over from various sewing or crafts projects. You can easily recycle this material by making beautiful flowers to accent a garment, hat, or hair, or use as party favors, gifts, decorations, or centerpieces.

I never dreamed of making flowers until I saw what rug hookers create from their scraps: proddy flowers. They're simply short pieces of wool that are "prodded" or pushed through canvas backing.

Skills I had learned in the past flowed back into my hands as I tried to create interesting leaves and accent flowers to enhance the old proddy designs. As I shared my samples with other rug hookers, we realized that almost anyone with a bare minimum of sewing knowledge could also enjoy making them. Plus, they are so simple, you don't need patterns!

The "How To" section is at the beginning of this book, followed by lots of photos showing how you can combine these techniques into a finished flower.

Have fun!

# Techniques

# Fabrics

$\mathcal{A}$ll the material used in this book is felted, woven wool recycled from clothing or cut from a bolt of fabric. Mid-weight scraps are perfect, but you can also use lightweight and heavy coat-weight wool. Try experimenting with thin handmade felt or recycled lightweight sweaters.

Empty out your closet, or visit resale shops and rummage sales to find slacks, skirts, and casual blazers. Buy only colors you love! Avoid dress suits, since their texture is not appropriate for making flowers. Check inside the garment for the "100% Wool" label.

Machine wash the clothes and fabric in hot water. To avoid vast amounts of fluff, do not cut apart any garment before washing. Just remove the shoulder pads if they are huge (they retain a lot of water) and buttons if they are special, then toss the garment in the washer, lining and all. Use a small amount of detergent and avoid softeners and conditioners.

Machine dry everything until it is hot and shrinks. Cut the clothes apart, tossing out waistbands, collars, heavily-interfaced sections, and linings. Some interfacings can be pulled off easily, and some hems can be ripped open. You will end up with soft wool ready to use.

Do not store your prepared wool in plastic bags—fold and store on an open shelf, keeping it in uncovered plastic or cardboard boxes. The wool should breathe a little. Don't worry about critters like clothing moths. They only like to eat dirty or smelly fabric.

Later, you may decide you want additional colors. You can easily dye over light-colored wool fabric with wonderful results. Just purchase basic red, blue, yellow, and black dyes suitable for wool (I use ProChem). Use a formula book (I use *Primary Fusion*) to create myriad hues. Be sure to be read and follow all instructions, as dye powders can be toxic.

# Supplies

# Basic Flower Pin

For a basic flower pin, you may have most of what you need already at your fingertips:

- Fabric scraps
- Sharp scissors/Rotary cutter
- Tacky glue or other thick white glue
- Needle
- Thread
- Pin backs
- Buttons, beads, trims

# Complex Flowers

For leaves, accent flowers, or more complex flowers, you may also need:

- Needle-nose pliers (with wire cutter)
- Floral tape
- #22 or #20 stem wire
- #22 or #20 cloth-covered stem wire

Proddy flowers also require rug canvas and narrow wool strips or yarn for hooking the centers.

# Basic Flowers

## Color

Choose your prettiest colors! Select solids and textures, such as plaids, tweeds, checks, and herringbone patterns, in coordinating colors. Use pastels for spring, bright summer hues, or deep autumn tones.

## Cut & Rip

Grab a 12- to 18-inch length of wool fabric with one straight edge. Rip off a strip about $1^1/2$ inches wide. Yes, rip it off—start with a short nick of the scissors, and rip!

## Sew

With a needle and thread to match the fabric, sew $^1/8$-inch-long stitches along the cut edge of the strip (not the edge you just ripped). Your stitches will be hidden by gathers, so don't worry about keeping them straight and even.

Gather the fabric as you stitch along the entire length, pushing the wool neatly along the sewing line, then knot the thread securely and cut the excess off.

Roll up the flower tightly, keeping the bottom edge even. Pass a long needle and thread through all the layers near the gathered stitches to secure the flower, making crisscross stitches across the flower bottom. If you like the ragged look, pull off a few more threads from the top edge. You're almost finished with your first flower!

To keep it simple, just attach a pin back: turn to page 25 for instructions. You can see some finished flowers created this way on pages 30–33.

Or you can add some leaves and buds, as shown in the next section. See page 34 for an example.

## Variations

By varying the length and width of the strips you use, you can achieve different results.

Try a different fabric, and cut another length. This time, push the gathers very tightly along your sewing line. Finish as before, and you will see how the shape opens out more fully than before.

Trim a very wavy shape, grading it from 1 to 2½ inches high. Save the leftover piece to make another flower.

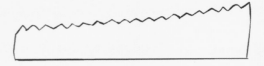

Use pinking shears or a rotary cutting tool with an interesting blade. (Avoid tools designed for use with paper—they may not be sturdy enough to cut cloth.) Cut large points or create half-moons.

For very showy flowers, cut deep scallops, $1/2$ to $3/4$ inch wide, from strips about $1\frac{1}{2}$ inches wide and 18 to 24 inches long. An example can be found on page 35.

Rather than roll up a gathered strip, shape it into a flat circle and glue in a button or yo-yo (see page 20) to hide the stitches, as the photos on pages 37–39 illustrate.

Patterns are not necessary for these flowers.

Be aware of how you are trimming shapes, and strive for smooth edges. Use the entire length of your scissors, moving the fabric towards the blades as you cut, and avoid tiny snip-snip-snips.

For wonderful shading, use hand-dyed, six-graded colors. These are predyed strips of wool fabric sold at rug hooking supply shops. Rug hookers like to shade flowers they create for rugs, so dyers supply six tones of the same color, ranging from light to dark. Start with the darkest shade in the center, and work out. Gather enough fabric of a single color to go around the flower completely, creating good balance.

Observe fresh flowers for more design ideas.

# A Fringe for a Daisy

Make small cuts in a 1-inch wide, 6- to 8-inch long strip to make a fringe. Make a flower center from a scrap of contrasting wool $1/8$ to $1/4$ inch wide and 3 inches long. Knot the middle and leave the tails hanging loose. Holding the tails of the knot tightly with one hand, roll the bottom, uncut edge of the fringe tightly around the knot with your other hand. Sew through all the layers when finished. Trim the knot's tails even with the rest of the flower.

The photos on pages 40, 41, and 43 show what you can create with this technique. You can use a scrap of heavy coat-weight fabric for a sturdy daisy. Small accent daisies are cute—experiment with them! Try trimming the tips of the petals to points or half moons.

## Different Shapes, Same Methods

Cut 1-inch-high triangles or half circles, overlap them, stitch through all the layers, and gather and roll up the fabric as before.

You can also cut graduated sizes of petals, keeping them in pairs on opposite sides of the basic shape, and overlap them, carefully stitching them into place as you go, to create a rose shape as pictured on page 64.

## Circle Shapes

Create four or five circle templates in $1/2$-inch increments, with the largest circle about 3 inches in diameter. You can trace around a large spool of thread, the bottom of a mug, a jar, a cosmetic container, or whatever else is on hand.

Use pinking shears or a wavy rotary cutter, or create scallops as you cut out the circle shape. Try clipping into the circle to create petals. Color-graded wool works well for these flowers; use the darkest hue for the smallest shape. You can also use patterned fabrics in coordinating colors.

Layer the circles and stitch a button, pearl, large bead, or yo-yo in the center, sewing through all the layers. If needed, add some glue between the layers. For more dimension, take small gathering stitches around the center and hide them under a button.

Examples of this kind of flower are pictured on pages 44 and 45.

## More Circles

Cut four or five shapes 2 inches in diameter from fabrics with similar tones. Fold and layer them into an interesting design. Hand-stitch them together, being sure to match the thread color to the color of the top fabric. You can also use white glue to attach the circles to each other, but be sure glued areas do not show through on the top. Take a look at the flower on page 68 for an idea using triangles and other shapes instead of circles.

## Proddy Flowers

Rug hooking rose to popularity in the late nineteenth to early twentieth centuries, when burlap became widely available; it is still a popular craft today. People cut used wool clothing into narrow strips and, using a hook, pulled loops up through the burlap to create rugs.

Short scraps of leftover fabric are put to use in creating "proddy" flowers: the fabric is "prodded" or pushed through the backing. See the photos on pages 50 and 51.

You can also "hook" a flower using long narrow strips of wool fabric or yarn. See the examples on pages 48 and 49. Visit a local rug hooking studio to purchase wonderful woolen fabrics, and use the studio's cutting machine to obtain some narrow strips. The #3 cut, or $^3/_{32}$-inch wide, is versatile. Complete directions on how to make proddy flowers are available in rug hooking books.

For both methods, you can use needlepoint canvas, monk's cloth, or linen canvas as a backing.

To keep the canvas from fraying once your flower is complete, run a bead of thick white glue around the edge of the reverse side then trim off the excess when dry.

The photo on page 55 shows a nickel-sized flower center hooked into linen canvas. Glue or hand-stitch five to ten 1-inch-high petals around the hooked center, folding a pleat in each petal. Be sure to avoid getting glue on the hooked loops!

# Leaves

## Color

Spring greens are brighter than summer leaves. Include leaves cut from yellow hues of green and blue-green shades for variety. Mottled, textured, hand-dyed wool is perfect. Autumn colors are rust, gold, and purple. Try deep brown and charcoal for winter. Try to use three or more different colors of leaves for each flower.

## A Simple Leaf

Patterns are not at all necessary to create a simple leaf! Just read the next few lines before you get your scissors ready . . .

Start with a strip of green wool 2 inches wide and 8 to 12 inches long, or a large scrap. Left-handed people will start at the left side of the strip, right-handed people at the right:

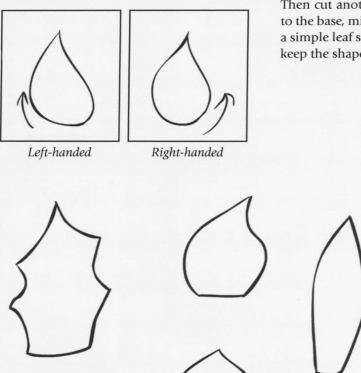

*Left-handed*          *Right-handed*

Look at one of the leaf shapes below, then slowly cut out the shape, starting at the base of the scrap, about 1 inch from the edge. Use the entire length of the scissors, cutting a curve up to the tip of the leaf. Then cut another curve from the tip down to the base, mirroring the first side, to create a simple leaf shape. This is easy to do if you keep the shape you want in mind.

Don't try to make the two sides of the leaf match exactly, and make each leaf slightly different. Make a few leaves from different scraps, and try different sizes and shapes. Go outside and collect a few small leaves to look at their shapes. Long, narrow leaves need to be stabilized with a short length of fabric-covered stem wire glued to the reverse side.

You can make your leaves fancier by clipping notches in the edges, gluing on lighter-colored veins of narrow wool strips, or gluing a light half-leaf over a dark half. You can also use pinking shears or a rotary cutter on the edges.

# A Stitched Leaf

With needle and thread matching the leaf color, just hand-sew ⅛-inch-long stitches along the bottom of a triangle, gather, and tie off.

For more depth, cut a rectangle, then fold the tips of the corners down to form a triangle and proceed as before.

# Winter Sprigs

Sprigs of spruce, pine, and fir are a bit more complicated. Using light, medium, and dark shades, cut three parallelograms along a 45-degree angle to the weave of the fabric, about ½ to ¾ inch wide and 3 inches long.

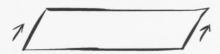

Stack the three layers and, with green thread, whip-stitch one long side, starting ½ inch from the top and leaving one end open about ½ inch. You can also run a thin bead of glue along one long edge between the layers.

Very carefully, cut thin slices into ³/₄ of the unit to make needles. Cut with the weave of the cloth, making strips only three or four threads wide to create the narrow needles. To prevent twisting, you may need to glue a length of #20 stem wire into the seam. The flower on page 61 is accompanied by a sprig of pine needles.

## Finishing

To create lively movement, pinch one or two leaves at their bases and carefully insert #20 or #22 stem wire (cut to 5 inches long). Fold down and twist tightly. Wrap with green floral tape.

For stability, some large leaves may also need a short length of wire glued to their backs.

# Accent Flowers

## Color

The brightest hues from your stash of small scraps make great accents for a corsage.

## Cut

Cut a 1-inch-high pie-wedge shape and roll it up into a cone. Secure with a dot of glue and run a wire through the base, or enclose it with a leaf or two and wrap with floral tape.

You can make another kind of accent flower by cutting four petal shapes from a small square and twisting a wire through the center.

You can make a pair of petals by cutting curvy points on both short ends of a ½ by 1-inch wool rectangle. Fold two pairs of petals in half, put a piece of wire through the center, twist, then tape.

You can also wrap buds inside a pair of leaves for cute party, wedding, or shower favors.

Fold a circle in half then roll it into a curvy shape. Run a piece of wire through the base, twist the wire together, and wrap it with floral tape.

## Yo-Yos

The historical shapes—circles folded to resemble one half of a yo-yo—were used extensively in the 1930s for bed coverlets. Here is an easy way to adapt them for a flower: eliminate the hem!

Start with a circle shape twice as large as the finished size you want—1½ to 2 inches in diameter works well. You can get a nice circle by using a fine-tipped permanent marker to draw around a small container lid or spool of thread onto the right side of the wool fabric. Trim off the inked line when you carefully cut out the circle, turning the fabric as you cut to obtain a smooth edge.

Hand-stitch around the perimeter, $^1/_8$ inch from the raw edge, gather tightly, and tie off. Use this as a flower center, with the raw edges up, or as a flower by itself by drawing it up loosely and adding a button to the center.

The photo on page 61 features a yo-yo flower.

## *Versatile Waves*

It is easy to make these from 1-inch uneven square shapes. Insert 4 inches of #22 stem wire through the center, push a seed bead over the wire, bend the wire down about $^1/_2$ inch, pushing it through the fabric again, then press the wires tightly together, and twist. Wrap with floral tape.

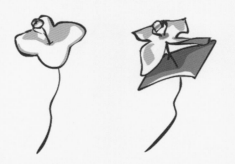

These types of flowers are shown on pages 66 and 75.

You can also make these flowers a bit larger. Think of a round jigsaw puzzle piece as you cut. Clip one or two threads at the center. Take a 3-inch strip of $^1/_8$- to $^1/_4$-inch-wide fabric (or a piece of yarn) and knot the center. With the tip of your scissors, needle-nose pliers, or a knitting needle, push both ends of the knotted wool or yarn through the tiny hole in the wool scrap, leaving the knot on top. You can secure this with a tiny dab of white glue on the bottom side. Trim the tails so they hide under the flower—or make them long enough to serve as an accent. You'll see these shapes on pages 69 and 70.

For another variation, layer two different sizes of cut-out flower shapes and forget the knot! Put a bit of glue between the layers and add a jewel or button to the top, as shown on page 75.

And for yet another option, make the knot larger than the flower. The flower on page 60 is an example.

The possibilities are endless, and that's what's fun about being creative with wool. Ask yourself, "What happens if? . . ."

## Calyx

Flowers look finished and buds defined when you add small green leaves as a calyx. The easiest way is to cut a small diamond or star shape, push it up a twisted wire to the base of a flower, overlap it over the flower base a bit, and glue it in place. Finish with wrapped floral tape. Out of tape? Use a narrow strip of wool!

## Pods and Berries

These little wonders are cute! Cut around a nickel or quarter. Hand-stitch around, 1/8 inch from the edge, stuff with tiny wool scraps, and pull the thread tightly, creating a ball shape. Wrap the base tightly with wire, add a calyx, then glue and wrap with floral tape. The photo on page 62 has a red pod.

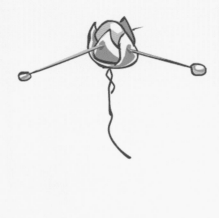

# *More Decorations*

Tendrils! On a piece of aluminum foil or thick plastic wrap, brush/sponge Stiffy, Modge Podge, or white glue over narrow wool strips or pieces of yarn about 5" long. Wrap them around a pen, plastic straw, knitting needle, or crochet hook, and let dry overnight. They add a certain spring to a flower, especially in chartreuse.

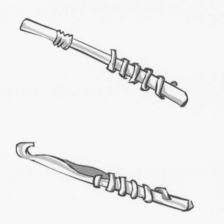

While you are getting glue everywhere, you might as well grab some brown scraps suitable for cinnamon sticks. Cut them into 3-by-1$\frac{1}{2}$-inch rectangles, glue them, and roll them up! There's a cinnamon stick on page 62. You can also glue then twist 3-inch lengths of narrow wool strips in shades of brown, green, and gold into the look of dried grasses or other plant materials for additional accents.

Narrow wool strips, yarn, raveled linen fibers, and so on make fine bows that can add a special touch to your design.

# How to Make Pins

# A Single-Flower Pin

If you want to keep it simple, just glue one flower to the front of the pin. First, from a scrap of wool fabric in any color, cut a circle or oblong large enough to just cover the base of a flower—about $1\frac{1}{2}$ to 2 inches. Cut two tiny slits, about $\frac{1}{8}$ inch long, in the circle, far enough apart for the ends of the pin back to fit through them. Open the pin back and insert each end through a slit, then close it. The pin should be on the right side of the cloth and the bar on the wrong side.

Squeeze craft glue onto the wrong side of the circle and then press your flower onto the glue. Push the flower down firmly and check the back (the pin side) to remove any excess glue.

# A Multiple-Flower Arrangement

Try out various leaves, buds, and other embellishments around the central flower. Contrast or match colors and hues to your satisfaction. This step is very enjoyable, and it is interesting to see how colors and sizes interact with each other. You can slightly bend wired stems into certain positions and fold waves in the leaves to offer more dimension.

Try for three points of interest around a central flower. You might put a leaf or two at eleven o'clock, a small bud at two o'clock, and two more leaves at six o'clock, for example. A bow looks best at the bottom or at a 2 o'clock position. Just show the leaves peeking out from under the flower. You can also position three smaller flowers in a triangle shape and add leaves around them. The shapes of the three flowers should vary.

Squeeze thick white glue onto a round wool base large enough to hold all the pieces. Place your selection of leaves (wrong side down) on the glue, with the bases of the leaves supported by the wool circle. Squeeze additional glue onto the leaves as necessary, if they will be covered by a flower. Next, glue on any accent buds or flowers and, finally, the central flower. Push everything down firmly and turn the entire piece over to the back side. Tuck in or trim edges and carefully wipe off any excess glue. Be sure both sides look neat and finished. Let dry overnight, then admire your creation and start making another flower! Everyone you know will want one!

## Corsage

You can select only wired flowers and buds and twist them into one unit to make a corsage, with stunning results! Add a corsage pin or hat pin to secure it onto a hat band, a piece of clothing, or a gift.

## Hair Ornament

Rather than attaching a pin back to your flower, glue a round or oval woolen base to the backs of the flowers. Then cut a strip of wool wide enough to fit on the base, make a fine line of glue on either long edge, and glue to the back, leaving enough space between the glued-down edges for a headband or barrette to slide through.

You can glue a long ribbon to the finished back instead and use it to tie the flower onto barrettes, gifts, potpourri jars, candles (don't let it burn!), wreaths, and so on.

# Flower Gallery

*This small white flower was made from the seam allowance of a blazer. It is glued onto a frayed scrap of linen rug hooking canvas.*

*Scallops were cut into strips of lilac and burgundy hand-dyed wool to make this flower.*

*Ripped, frayed wool strips become flowers when gathered with easy hand sewing.*

*Simple leaves accent this very simple flower made from a length of hand-dyed, frayed wool.*

*Confidence and a large hat are all you need to wear this hand-dyed purple flower with scalloped edges. Magenta leaves were added for contrast.*

*Pale green hues from hand-dyed wool, carefully cut with deep scallops, form this pastel flower.*

A single strip of wool was dyed yellow on one side and green on the other and gathered up the middle, between the two colors. The bottom layer of another piece of yellow wool adds depth.

*A circle was appliquéd to the top of a wavy circle embroidered with French knots. It was then glued to a slightly ruffled hand-dyed blue-green strip.*

This flower is simply two layers of gathered strips topped with green clipped shapes. The leaves are folded rectangles.

*A cluster of buttons accents a wavy circle glued to a scalloped, gathered piece of hand-dyed fabric.*

*This fringed blue strip was wrapped around a knot and secured with thread. The large leaf was gathered slightly with hand-sewn stitches.*

This linen hatband features 1-inch flowers and leaves appliquéd with linen raveling. Narrow wool strips serve as ties. A separate matching pin with three flowers secures the band to the hat.

*This pin combines colorful variations of flowers in small sizes.*

*Here is another small pin combining different kinds of small
flowers.*

*Layered circles are easy to clip and shape. These are topped with a button stitched on through all the layers.*

*After cutting small sections in the edges of layered circles, you can cut scallops.*

The white center of this flower was hooked through linen canvas. A circle was cut out from the center of a coral hand-dyed scrap just large enough to fit around the white base. Darker coral touches were glued on separately. Small accent flowers are 1-inch wavy circles punched with knots.

*A circle of white coat-weight wool was trimmed to resemble large petals then attached to a pointed and gathered red strip with a button.*

*Various heights of hooked wool strips are glued to a single scrap of green wool cut out in leaf shapes.*

*Here is another flower made of hooked wool strips in various heights.*
*The green accent is a circle folded in half and shaped.*

This periwinkle proddy flower with a hooked center is trimmed with leaves, buds, and a curly tendril.

*The ragged edges and bud on this proddy flower give it an informal look.*

*This sunflower, 6 inches in diameter, is created with three hues of gold intermingled.*

*Four hues of purple were hooked around a center that's hooked in three shades of brown to suggest movement.*

*Heavily textured fabric works well for making flowers. The textured red strip was gathered and sewn around a hooked center.*

*Orange petals were glued around a hooked center. The wool acorn accents this autumn-colored flower nicely.*

The chartreuse accents complement this deeply scalloped purple flower. Note the richly textured, frayed scrap glued next to a leaf. The narrow two-tone leaves accompanying this flower are wired on the back to keep them stiff.

*Three different fabrics are deeply scalloped and twisted around each other to create this pinecone.*

*The camel fabric is accented with a wool Japanese lantern and bright hand-dyed oak leaf.*

*Layered plaid circles make up this winter flower. The pine sprig was sewn from three layers of fabric.*

*These barrettes feature purchased red berries and wavy circles glued to a base.*

To make a cinnamon stick like the one in this pin, just roll up a glued
rectangle of brown wool and let it dry.

*This large plaid proddy is accented with a stuffed wool yo-yo, cinnamon stick, and plaid holly leaves.*

*Daffodils are made by gluing petals to a circle and topping it off with a tube. When dry, glue a #20 fabric-wrapped wire to the back and add narrow leaves.*

*A simple rose is made from pairs of petals shaped around each other.*

*This center of this calla lily is a strip of yellow wool glued around a wire.*

*These lilies of the valley are larger than the real thing. Gather a short strip at the top to form the flower, then turn the top inside out and sew or glue the edge.*

*Layered triangles and squares, with simple triangle leaves, give a*
*contemporary look. They are sewn together with a narrow strip of wool.*

*Glue shapes of wool together or attach them with a button to create a simple layered flower with no stitches showing.*

These hair ties are made from
I-cords knitted from chunky yarn
and accented with a wavy circle
with a knot in the center.

*These barrettes are decorated with simple flowers made from wavy circles.*

To create an initial, fuse interfacing to the reverse side of a wool scrap. Then cut the letter out from the scrap and glue it to the backing. You can also use a product such as Heat'n Bond instead of interfacing and iron the letter onto the backing.

*Like to iron? Purposeful pleats can turn a plain piece of wool into a flower.*

*Tiny buds like these can be used as party favors.*

*Look for scraps in interesting shapes—like this bit of yellow wool, which was left over from cutting out daffodil petals.*

*Gather three sizes of wavy circles in the center, then layer them. To make
the tiny accent flowers, push a fabric-covered stem wire (#20 or #22)
through two wavy circles and make a tiny twist of wire to secure them.*

# Acknowledgments

*T*he fabrics used in the flowers on pages 34, 35, 37, and 75 were dyed by Nancy Blood of Owego, New York. Thanks to Della Griffiths, of Pittsburgh, Pennsylvania, for the dyeing class. Friends Carolyn, Marsha, Marlene, Nancy, Meredith, Bernie, Audrey, Doris, Diane, Marion, and Marilyn Grant and Joanne Horansky (now deceased) offered tremendous encouragement during sessions with the Laurel Mountain Rug Hookers at St. Paul's, Trauger, Pennsylvania. Thanks to the staff, volunteers, docents, and shoppers at the Westmoreland Museum of American Art in Greensburg, Pennsylvania, for their valuable support. Kim Kiser, your drawings are awesome, and thank you for your help! Deb Smith, *Rug Hooking* magazine editor, thanks for creating the opportunity; and Mark Allison and Kathryn Fulton, at Stackpole Books, you made it happen! Thank you. Heartfelt thanks to Ric for putting up with the mess and vacuuming when it gets too thick!